mother tongues

# mother tongues

POEMS

TSITSI ELLA JAJI

NORTHWESTERN UNIVERSITY PRESS
EVANSTON, ILLINOIS

Northwestern University Press
www.nupress.northwestern.edu

Printed in the United States of America

10   9   8   7   6   5   4   3   2   1

Library of Congress Cataloging-in-Publication Data
Names: Jaji, Tsitsi, author.
Title: Mother tongues : poems / Tsitsi Ella Jaji.
Description: Evanston, Illinois : Northwestern University Press, 2020.
Identifiers: LCCN 2019033105 | ISBN 9780810141353 (trade paperback) |
    ISBN 9780810141360 (ebook)
Classification: LCC PS3610.A385 A6 2020 | DDC 811/.6—dc23
LC record available at https://lccn.loc.gov/2019033105

*for Tembo Jamel, who took root here*

## OUR LINGERING EMBRACE

lifted us above the whipping winds:
we turned into a banner. Shoulder draped
over shoulder, we knotted neck to crooked neck,
and so we became the net that broke each other's
fall. Between us, a common tongue took root—
its song: full-throated trust. Where elsewhere
fist on fist of plagues would bruise our hide,
our inmost sanctum stood blemish-free.
Tender was our fortress.          Once, we were one solid bloc
                                  of granite, bold as marble.
                                  Now we swivel and
float on air like dancers, watching wonder
marble: the you in me, the me in you,
our living monument, this only child.

# CONTENTS

## MOTHER TONGUE

mother of two, mixed-and-matched Ohio blonde brings
her brown babies—born to a brand-new nation—home
alone. cash-strapped, father of two stays behind, husbanding
their shared hearth. she tames the air-bound toddler boy

on an elastic leash. in the airport, an unknown wasp-waist girly-
woman squawks in alarm: her blessedly untested parental principles.
when boy won't budge, his corduroy seat sails across the waxed
floors while sister does dragging duty, a trail of gleam in their wake.

that sister's bush-born vernacular follows this proven logic:
with mother, speak mommy's talk, otherwise, be at home in words.
father-less for a spell, her tale of ups and downs and pressure and
vomit in a paper bag wells up at the sight of the first matching man.

> Black is beautiful: powered by pride,
> wounded with each stop, blunted by each frisk.
> Black is the color of our first true love,
> baba, warm heart beating to calm colic,
> nightmares, and memory's flicker of
> something history will call *Chimurenga*.

the language of home spills off daughter's tongue, drowning this
unknown umber man whose skin is a flag of peace. his face laughs,
bewilders, then unsettles in dread: white woman/panic/will bring
only trouble. he harbors no desire for the body of this bronze girl-
child/no bribe/no candy/no white van out back. suddenly, he sees
they look like *family*, yet he can sight no ocean to wash them apart.

mother knows best: *so sorry*
mother knows best. she clasps small
brown hand in hers, and smooths golden
head of spiral hair with a free hand;

she spells out a new code: *everyone here*
*speaks only mother's tongue.*
now sister does too.
end of story.

# OUR MOTHER OF STONE

The cushion of her flesh is veiled in lichen.
Where her breasts once gave way
she is rough to the touch. Crowned

with a pot of water, her eyes drop dead
as the tail of the double-chinned lizard.
Queen of Heaven, she aches for nothing now.

She props the Absolute's illusionist
upon her hardened lap. Her chin quivers;
her belly too, recalling this wild fruit's flight.

Clouds of sulphur pass for seraphim. Heaven
greens over like the beady eye of a magnate
tracking sooty children who flee his coins.

Every frontier is blocked, so Our Lady lifts the runaways
into her tender choke-hold. The rich fume, empty-handed:
swindled of thread, and those cheap, nimble little fingers.

## ON THE ISLE OF LESBOS

*for the ones who welcomed refugees on the Aegean shores*

Months later, the island's sheep
shuffle, uneasy with silence. Last year
a hundred thousand voices begged to be
buried here, not in Aleppo. They retched
as if heaving could save them. But only
thick seas of salt spilled onto the holiday

sand. Now an island man clenches his jaw.
The earth holds his only daughter still.
One Christmas, spasms seized her. The next,
her brother shook his way to lay down beside her
body below. Then this fishing man learned
what grave diggers already know, by doing.

Only the boat's lip remained, trembling on a crest
of sympathy. He moored himself in his nets: a morning
haul of squid mimed hope. Then the tide turned:
his arms flooded full of other men's
children, come to rescue him
from an unfathomed ocean of grief. Mothers'

mothers were caught off guard. They shepherded this
off-season crowd to the guesthouses, fed them ewe's
milk, took care to pay their stumps no mind.
These sibyls already knew—from Turk, from Greek—
how opposites can hurl their waves of rage at
no-man's-land, and turn men and women to ruins.

If they had it to do over again, they would,
and could, now that their villages have cleared,
now that the boy's photograph has won
its Pulitzer and slipped our minds. They feel washed

out, they feel their memories ebb. Their faint,
faded Sapphic rags must have been drowned out

by Madeira's sirens, and Ibiza's disco scene.
Once a day, a woman sights a tiny ghost
toddling across the water. All that these
islanders have earned is anxious rest.
Not even saints, stranded at home, can live without
bread to kiss and milk to rinse it from their lips.

# DAUGHTERING

*for my father, who remembers only what matters*

When the dune crests, she finds she has too much body left. To reach
the drowning fields she will have to shed muscle, shear breasts, cap off
her boyhood. This banter must shrivel into a loop of repeating wind rush,
while the stutterer insists his thought would resurrect if only the other words

would be still. She thinks her thighs have doubled, so she pours them
down the drain. Now is the time to carry only what fits on her spine.
There is more than one way to become an Amazon.
If she plans to outlast the burials she must level with the panther

who deserted her before it showed her how to bare teeth. On the hunt,
it always claimed the lightest foot, the surest kill. But this is madness:
what stalks them now is not silence but memory's sloth, giving its all
away. She will need to stay here, fix her eyes. First

she must ease the steering wheel into the grave. She will need to stop
wanting for time, stop fussing at what snaps or fumbles.
When the wave crests it litters silt, not gold. It was never going to
end that way. Wealth feeds on decay, like loam.

To walk them away from the proof of that first Florida banana tree
will be the true ruin: to lay sack to a rhizome of roots, to grant neither
net nor fountain sway, to give away the bed to the wrong person,
to discover the table is unwanted, the cloth, too,

unwanted, the cactus celebrating the wrong season.
There will be nothing left to make a gift of.
Still, she comes to share the pall, with eyes like stones.
Her spine must be her only flask. She sees

the wisdom of black veiling lace. She sees
there was never enough water:
the sandy crest broke long before
the first prophet lit up her hair. This is love.

## AND THEY DIDN'T DIE

*for my mother, who has done all things well*

I bring a squall of quiet, my hectoring force, to shame
the belated fog of orders and bandages into a fine mist.

I am here to squelch reason's panic. Certainty
is scrambled and we find only Vaseline, thick with scent,
and too heavy to churn the waters. If they wept no tears
they would not know I will not shed any.

If there were no tremors they would not know me. Unshaken.
I will outlive them. I will bury them in my question: What more?


This is what we have done since before
the border between wild and free was pinned

like steel and plaster, animal and woman, birth
and death. Only daughters are shouldered
into becoming Mother, cold
without children, colder still after birth.

This is how it has always been.
All we cannot know is when.

# IN PRAISE OF THE GREAT CAT

*for Ambuya Jaji and her totem, Shumba Nyamuzihwa*

Today I have come begging wisdom of the cat.
Cowed by messages my body leaves in code,
it is her flex I crave, to ease the arduous distance
between arch and heel. Beneath her I feel
a hum, alongside the pump of heart unhurried
except in sympathy with mine. Her eyes—
banks of pooled sunlight—
look into mine.      She asks nothing.
She is all here. I have never seen her lips,
but her tongue unsmooths my hair,
forgives my disarray, stretches all.
O, spirit of my grandmother, friend of my youngest self,
come to me in each body you have chosen.
You have stayed by me, quickened calm, then sprung away.

## LINGUA: CORRAL

       *the lips*
               *the teeth*

                      *the tip,*
                            *the tongue*

# FIVE BAGATELLES

*after Beethoven, for Malcolm Bilson*

## Opus 27, Number 2 (The Moonlight Sonata)

In its fullness,
a Hungarian touch sent
the fortepiano's wooden
teeth clattering to the floor.

\*

## Opus 2, Number 3

Once, the golden boy fell through a chair.
It looked like magic. The trick: his corduroys
cloaked a peg-leg that suddenly came
unhinged. Wads of apologies tumbled

across the master class—
a rush of mutterings about
glue, round pins, and, *ach*,
the squared wicker.          By the time

we were eating dainties
and pointing out slurs
in the score, he was all dusted off,
propped up and smug as a bug, again.

\*

## Opus 101

I wonder if the orchids are there
for good form or

for *Empfindsamkeit*—
two stacks of pink,

one lily-gloved, one puckered lime.
As counterpoint, a cyclamen
soaks up claret, as from
a decanter.

\*

## Opus 53 (*The Waldstein*)

There are only two ways
to choose your favorite note.
Always prefer the highest.
And if not, simply
admit you're wrong. *Emphatically.*

\*

## Opus 111

The pulse, the dainties, the
*Urtext*, and the rotting keys
add up to that one difference:
the high or the low.

Each week the maestro sighs
at accents, sloth, and clipped quavers.
But first he arches a mustached brow
and shrugs, "It's very good, you know."

His mornings are spent campaigning
to mute dinner music in restaurants,
so we can finally eat like the deaf,
in peace. O, dona nobis pacem.

# FINGERINGS

*after Robert Schumann dies down*

Feeling the way back
to a face         I can face,
mind wracked for words,
shame is what I know best.
Only its name escapes me.

Robert, my own slow man,
I think you called this freezing point
*Eusebius.* Or is it a name I call myself,
a yes,   see,      ache—
after sitting my own nine night?

I remember every episode,
and that wonder—sharp
miracle of March—each time
the season out of reach
is finally out of reach.

That is the octave I am reaching for when I play *mas.*

# FLARE

*after Robert Schumann's long gone*

Every once in a while,
our modern rhythms
call in our bluff,
that pound of
flesh.

Then we must own
up to who we are.
Shy, locked within
our rooms, we lay us
down to rest.

# SYMPHONY BOARD DINNER WITH PIANO SOLOIST

*for Vladimir Feltsman, maestro*

After the octaves of Beethoven Op. 58, muscle memory remembers nothing
feels better than, bone in hand, fat trickling down the chin. The trick is
to catch the fur-lined ladies at table, grab the meat from under their snub
noses, taste it before it is forked or knifed, and suck out the marrow of
tradition. We come to steal back what Mr. T. S. Eliot stole. We come red,
feathered, and tarred. We will have seconds. Fistfuls please us more than
niggardly dainties.

## BLUE NOTE

*for Guy Ramsey, maestro*

Lord, make me an instrument.
I am no fool.                                Hard hands
made tools of us.
If I had a hammer—.

If there's a balm to make us whole,

                                       make it
night time,                                  the right time
to turn spiritual. Lord,

all the balm I have is                       me.
What song I make is                          me.
Lord, make me                                like you.
Sometimes I feel

like I'm almost gone.                        What's
mine is patched and                          crooked:
cowpea rows, chicken feet, hog guts.
I'll make this song bend over                me.

I'll make it                                 wipe my brow.
                                             *Tenderly.*

## COOKING WITH MILES

Say you want to make a Pork Pie:
first off, take you a nice, plump ham
and slap it in the pan.
                    Don't give it long—
you don't want it getting too cute in there.

Yeah, you wanna stir that bitch up
like a drummer playin brushes.
                    Grease her up good.
Grease, mothafucka, you know what grease is
don't you? Shit. Now you threw me off.

O yes, next you need some flavor.
The hot five, I like to call them:
cayenne, chili powder, vinegar, and salt. And Old
Bay                    —That's a trick I picked up
at a crab boil in one them after-hour joints.

'Course salt's a spice, fool—
                    Where your people from?
Now the crust got to be
handled soft and gentle. Tenderly.
Get you some lard,

some flour,
some more salt,
some water—and some vodka. That's
my secret sauce, keeps things nice and loose,
for the perfect crust: blonde          and flaky.

## RELAXING WITH MILES

*trading fours with Jason Moran*


Never met anyone seem so much
like granite burning                 from the inside.

Jackie Battle, seven years.
Bless you my brother.

\*


The two largest heads I ever seen:
Al Sharpton                      and Muddy Waters.

Lonely? I get so lonely sometimes
I talk to an *apple*.

\*


His hair was so glorious;
His hair was so glorious

It had body

                     *and* soul.

\*


Honeysuckle Rose swamped Paris. And
all that tape was was James Brown.    —Mm.

That was a lesson right there, man:
silver sap and who you know.

## LINGUA: TONGUE-TIED

*clamped muscle, shell shutter:*
*hold fast to mum's*
*word, safe-boxed secret*
*perch, mothering a pearl.*

*seep salt, water's spell*
*of pucker potion, brewed*
*from crystals. land-locked,*
*who knows what swimmer's*
*ear called you here.*

*spasm's clutch, tight-lipped*
*as razors down below:*
*loosen when you will,*
*and admit that*
*one tongue that savors*
*your delectable might.*

## TELL ME SOMETHING GOOD

Who blessed the raucous cry of sparrows,
blaring out their call to prayer? As if
this grey were not, dead-tired, April's latest spit.
Who woke up this morning and, rose-shafted,
took light for a lucky charm, or worse, a
word from the Lord. Who, up at six, thinks
this is hope? Who can't afford to sleep?
When the radio croons, who slides on up,
hot body wired for a payday loan?
Who cannot smell the coffee yet? There's no
one coming to celebrate a skirted cliff,
a missing mark. Snow bleeds out on tarmac. Cut.
Slow clot to black. This is America. Now,

                          let me hear you sing.

# A SONG AT DAWN

*for Ngugi wa Thiong'o, father*

Grain-scatterer, we too have shed our apostolic alias
and followed you into the shade to hear our voices
bloom. Here *rapoko*, here *chibage*, here *zviyo*, here

*nzungu*, here *nhanga*, here sweet, sweet *nhope*.
Here a name we call ourselves.
Here a thing we will not do: steal, red-handed.

Grain-distributor, we trade words with you. We
give an *mbeu* here for a buried seed there. We
mark up the goods by candlelight, in blue or red

ink. We shrink with doubt from a place called
Nation. One thing we can say for sure: We will never be
a colony again. Need the obvious be stated this way?

Gainsayer, what would you ask us to ask now: What is dying
below the topsoil, that dusting of iron will, nitrous rage,
pot ash? What birthright is traded when a crow

lays her eggs in a crocodile's nest? What will translate this
longest century into a new election cycle, a conference
of women, men, young visionaries, and aging dreamers

debating under Wangari's forest of green umbrellas?
We will plough your plot, furrow its surface, burrow in the
tunnels of language. Our dismay is our hope, present at

every meeting. In simpler times the answers might have
slipped off our tongues. Now family feuds erupt into wars.
It seems these devilish thorns and eroded rock are also our

inheritance: these lands, these languages, these mother tongues.
You have left us no choice, O stubborn prophet of Gĩkũyũ,
but to try our tongue, and listen as silence softly

breaks.

# AUXILIARY

*for Angelika Kratzer, linguist*

*While it is not absolutely impossible,*
*it is nevertheless quite unlikely that Nature*
*could construct an angel*
*from an extant phylogeny.*

*The back of a mammal*
*has no preexisting structures*
*that can be stretched or shrunk,*
*folded or bent into a wing.*

*

These, then, are the concerns of
the Semanticists and their rival siblings,
the Syntacticians. They worry about
how to swansong a boat.

More precisely, they start with a boat.
Take a boat in Boston, for example.
Say, something like "swan boat."—But
they do not suppose we all know what that is.

"Is it a
*swan* boat, or
a swan *boat?*"
they might quibble.

Then, they really get going—
they suggest a "swan boat book"
and we twitter with erudite delight.
—They keep a straight face.

Well then, what about a
"Swan Boat Book Award"?—
and our snobbery is further
excited. Why, what would the

award ceremony look like?
What would we wear? Would we—
perhaps—break with our own traditions
and wear a dress?

Would we wear a pantsuit?
But who, besides a Swan Boat Book Awardee,
wears a pantsuit these days?
The striding syntactician has a twinkle in her eye.

Her angelic powers may be diminutive, but
her impishness is palpable, and for reasons
known only to her, she honors each of our traditions.
*Invoking Langston, she wins us over completely.*

*

This, then, is our best effort at last, our opening closer:
a cooperative interaction, we hope, in the spirit of such.
We present our sister semanticist (or was she a syntactician?)
with this salute, a swan song, after all. We hope it suits.

## PRELUDE TO A KISS

Under the water's skin
the mouth
is a handkerchief
sponging wet salts
that          wake          wonder.

Is this spilling eye
despair, or just
an answer
to smoke, old age,
a stray          grain          of sand?

Anemone. Anemone.

*

The mouth
is a fist
full of fingers.
Soft teeth drift
in the deep.

A sea-rose,
licked pink,
turns purple
in the limpid
cobalt blue.

Below the meniscus, things float:
          fingers,
          hands, cheek
          bones.
No push.          No pull.          No current.

Only water

                                  brushing a herd of medusas.

        Thick things—                          soft things,

                      smoothed

       by water.

Smoother
still,
petals spread in
wet, unmetered
breath.

Anemone. Anemone

*

Feeding on
each other's names,
the mouth
drowns, aleatoric,
in the eye.

*Anonynominehmen'aimenescianomali,*
*Neumannamnesiasinenomonemesistema,*

*Stameneenenymphominimaliaminanemone,*
*Moanimomaterailymitimimesimillenaria*

*anemonstrosillypsistah, nomemataminemonomême*
*simazisomyomendimensio. Dominamanimane*

*monodimelomaniamudiwamnesimilitude.*
*Anemonephylumcnidariacoelenteratantho*

*zoanematocyst. Anonymanemono*
*mi me nominanemone.*

Anemone.
Anemone.

## FIRST GUARDIAN OF FLIGHT:
### *THE ANGEL OF TIME*


Brown leathered feet
glide just behind

the foot traffic's beat.          Arresting—
doubled brown leather attaché,

unfairly matched against
unbended back.          His perfect grey

wingspan presses the jacket's
shoulder blades;          thin socks

look out as planned.
The brother's hand smooths

the hard shell's rare, rusted sailing.
This art of no disturbance—    a vermillion

halo shelters his ears. O, how he floats like a
brown moth, a          silence other travelers skirt

(stun-gunned into
Indian file).

## SECOND GUARDIAN OF FLIGHT:
### *THE ANGEL OF REFINEMENT*


washroom assistant in the Ladies'
also black/not from here

*hello honey/darling/sweetheart/*
*plenty of room very clean welcome*

to rush hour (alternate)
        flushing toilets butt in         back to

having *a lovely day a lovely day*
*a lovely day*         remember to say

*thank you for tips* /for peppermints
tampons/pads lotion.

                "Thank you so much."

## AFTER TONSURE

Afloat in God's ocean, a seam of light
frays the mounting clouds. Doubt
propels me, wings just out of view.

My knees ache. To stretch
would shame me, buckling the back
of a sleeping stranger.

I bottled no holy water from the pool in Dakar,
nor corked its early solitude. I flailed instead, a novice
to crawl, then panted in luxury on sandstone.

A noxious incense soared from opaque open canals.
I wondered who answers the Medina's muezzin,
swamped daily in this. Who hallows such a dawn?

Home is the other side of East, an ever brighter
desert. In a mirror I saw this cut was no good,
but beamed my thanks in retreat.

I reasoned with the stranger's freedom:
it will grow back, the better to be shorn.
What made this hour night? What makes this day new?

## LINGUA: LADYFINGERS

*science knows so little*
*of the algorithmic slurping*
*up of water. tongue*
*twist outpaces the camera*
*lens. desert cat turned*
*familiar drinks from glass*
*bowls; steals cream, snags*
*chicken breasts, laps up*
*rank pop-tops' contents.*
*sly, slick drinking buddy,*
*head-tamer, fur-soaker,*
*lip-licker, fickle fiend:*

*small wonder, we name*
*lost memories* cats' tongues.

## PROCEDURE FOR INITIATION INTO THE ZEBRA SISTERHOOD

Try to avoid the fool
who mistakes a zebra

for a pack mule. That fool
is probably a jackass.

Get too close and you may
get a kick in your nuts.

So: grow a pair,
and join the tribe.

## ETHIOPIA STRETCHES FORTH HER HANDS

I, sphinx,
Peace be upon you.
Hear the mother's plaint:
*is old enough to marry now,*

am Cheops.
Peace only.
*I passed my GCSE in 1986. My small boy*
*and I have never held a job. And neither has he.*

No sphinx before onions,
I sleep west of Tunisia,
The world is all atwitter.
Dear Lion of Alexandria!

I squint my pity:
but I wake with the sun.
Schisms open up.
Dear desert, O, dear Ra.

The land of immolation,
the placard's tight riddle:
and yet, who always ends
I ask you this:

the acrid waft of refusal,
I AM A MAN;
where she began?
Ain't I a woman?

## ELECTIONEERED (2013)

That mustache, more visible after the razor.
That face. That wry old joke about the rooster
whose cockled crow sounds less like a boast,
and more like Sunday dinner, before dinner.

Like a dog barking at the sun.
Like a rally that felt like a party.
Like the pall before the storm.
Like carrying a load on your head,
while seated in the bus. Like this
if you thought Baba Jukwa was more
than hot air piping out of Facebook.

Like anyone would feel if their face were plastered
everywhere, smacked across mothers' buttocks wrapped in
Zambia cloth, posted in all post offices, all schools, all hospitals.
*Change the dressing, sister*, you would say. *Let it all air out.*

Like how one feels
sometimes,
thinking about
that selective
assemblage:
history.

Like dawn, never new, never news.
Like when we . . .
Like when the When-We's whine:
*See, we told you.*

How a farm here and there,
an enemy or two, a car, a few mineshafts
account for haggard crimes against all humanity,
while mothers' mothers saw those When-We's

arriving with the gun, the bible,
and something short an inheritance.

*Little lord fauntleroys,*
*how you loved your kitchen boys,*
*gardening,*
*and serving tea*
*and yes-madamming.*

Toyi, toyi!

Ah, the great leader's
bicameral brain
is but the lonely
mind of one
who has out-
lived his heroes.
The ungentle goodnesses of night,
ah, the graceless airs of love.

The people
love the great leader, his excellency,
his honorable arch-comradeship.

The people love to see him thumb his nose
and toss great boogers at those buggers,
the bastard Brits. Admit it, then:

You love it, too.
You love it because
You do not need bread,

You do not need mealie meal,
You do not need sugar,
You do not need antiretrovirals,

You do not need a new wheelbarrow,
You do not need a prophet,
You do not need a bank to change

your null and void Zimkwachas
into wads of golden USAs,
You do not need a green card,

You do not need a place to hide,
You do not live here.
You do not live here anymore.

## OLD NEWS

### 1. #ThisFlag

Today we are flying colours:
black, red, white, green—
yellow's caution to the wind.


### 2. Quails

If this were the actual bread of heaven
would spaza shops be hawking it?

If a rooster lays a pangolin's egg
drop it and see if rubber cracks.


### 3. In the Garden of Gamatox

What are Organochlorine pesticides?
What do they look like?
Where do they come from?
Where can they be found?
Why are OCPs harmful?
What happens if they are not used as directed?
Do I have any OCPs on my property?


### 4. The Fountain of Youth

When you are
61 years young,
40 is the new 21.

## THE CRYSTAL RIVER

What a croc. This river
is the crooked line between
rand/dollar. Neither is ours.
We cannot even afford our own money.

This river plays the national pastime, hunger, like a champion.
This river wears our national dress, *nzara*, like a string of hip-beads.
This river teems with crocodiles evicted from their farm.
Now they are just swimming in the Wild Wild.

> To bury Ambuya
> send one thousand USAs
> for the morgue to release the body.
> It has cracked apart sincerity.
> Best to live far, far from the extortionist's ministries,
> the indefinite suspension of power,
> the reliable humiliation of hunger pangs,
> and subscribe to the national philosophy: remittance.

*Shall we gather by the river, the beautiful, the beautiful river?*

> Once there were *njuzu* swimming in the Limpopo,
> water spirits to charm but yes truly, to charm.
> They were the magical traces of spirit worlds
> I could graft myself into—
> their sirens were more beautiful and more serious than the
> revelations of
> Rev. Bitchington
> et al.
> Those *njuzu* might choose a favorite,
> whose morals would survive, floating intact.
> That favorite, maybe me, might wander lustily.

How this river has crossed us.
It has done what it was always doing: it has flowed.
It has overflowed.
It has flooded with crocodile's drool.
It has flushed bright crimson, a sea of severed limbs.

Ah, border hunger. Look at you.
You are just eating money, sitting there,
bedazzled in Capricorn's tropical light,
a muddy swirl to confound tourists.
You are just seated there, guzzling us down:
first our eldest, the one we ground *dovi* for so he could
sell peanut-butter sandwiches to raise bus fare,
then the daughter who did not tell us she was pregnant, nor by whom,
and now our old science teacher who can no longer afford transport to school.
O dark river of crystal, your hunger exceeds ours.
Your borders are more absolute, your demands more ravenous.
O Limpopo, you fisher of men, your flock
of women are disciples, bellies full of mud:
the rich you have sent emptying away,
across Beitbridge, to Plumtree, then Sun City.

But the true believe they will scrape by in the land of ExDorado.
They come with nothing noble in mind,
no moral edge, no ideological vision, no song.
Hunger is the bare banal.
Here, swimming with crocodiles,
we are among our own: all ravenous mouths,
all skin hardened into allegory,
all thiefs of the pronouns of others.

You did not have to cross the Limpopo to have severed limb from limb.
To remit love at the Western Union desk is no simple matter.

> *Do you want to know what they call a coloured in Shona?*
> Muzukuru, the child of your sister.
> They don't ask where it came from,
> they just integrate it into the family.

*So you want to know what they call a coloured in Shona?*
My friend, sometimes it is the child of your brother.
And it must learn how to do those things only
Sekurus or Maininis can do.
It cannot just be a muzukuru.
It cannot just be a secret keeping secrets,
shut out of the meeting place of adults.

Limpopo, border river, our very own Río Grande.
I cannot call this exile, but I do not know what else to call home.

# PROFILE

*for Memory Chirere, poet*


Our brother Memory has posted a picture of new plants
growing from the inside of the old. He has asked this picture
to stand in for him. The mouth of his brother Allen
waters at the thought of what there is to say about
a trunk whose core has gone to seed.

Or about what better options one might have chosen
than new wine and old skin. Maybe Allen hopes
Memory will capture in words what hope
feels like, or recall how the barrel of a blade of grass
tastes when you bite into it. Allen knows Memory

knows his way to the other side of deep Shona.
He knows what Memory can do with
an easy read, or book-learning on the edge
of unemployment, or a story in a land where a job
is an oddity. Allen knows that Memory knows

how to grow exactly what he wants, where he wants,
so long as it rains. But Memory knows that if the crops
are failing again and again, it might not be just new seed
we need. It might be that we should look again
at this harvest that has come to show us that what is old

cannot stop what is coming, cannot contain it,
cannot compress it, cannot elude it, cannot monitor it,
cannot settle it. What is coming may not be a tree, but
it may not be just weeds either. What it is, we cannot know.
We can only be sure that in the rot, something is rooting.

## AFTER THE COUP (OR NOT)

Some are dancing in broad daylight, in the street,
like before revolutions were televised,
when jokes were told out loud. I am watching

as if someone I loved was gravely ill, as if dancing
would damage the child I am carrying between
bouts of sleep and cynicism. It would appear that this

business of one passport and two homes has not worked
as well as I dreamed. One cellphone, 9 Western Unions,
12 news apps, and none of them reliable.

My cousin-brother sends pictures, on WhatsApp,
the kind a man paid out of his own pocket can afford.
His sister plies the road between her daughters' schools and

her own, reading as if knowledge could bridge the gap
between bond and dollar, bleak and bright, that and ours.
Our generation opens the messages, occasionally we

kikikiki in private, in Cape Town, or in North Carolina.
We know what looks fake, what is sassy, what is sloppy.
We know nothing. We say nothing. We have not been asked

to punt, to opine, to pronounce. We know
enough to know that what we read is not the whole story,
enough to know history makes better reading than news.

## HOW I WRITE

*for R. Ellis Neyra, poet*

Now, I see
that my wilderness
is our field,
and I call
my neighbor to
come plough it
with me. Our
hoes dig deep.

Our harvest spills
over into something
an awful lot
    like hope.

## LINGUA: GOOD TASTE

umami, *smack of this*
*millennium's silver teeth*
*and honey tongues*

## REAL SIMPLE

Scissors, fresh from the take.

It all makes perfect sense now. How original it seemed to cut dry things
—paper dolls with long sewing-pattern legs and boxes full of grown clothes.
How sensible to spend a hot, ripe afternoon indoors, in and out of dress.
I'm reading about women finding their aha moment, without even turning
Oprah on. It's all about keeping your canned tomatoes neat, controlling the
inevitable juices that run over the counter.

Give me a chignonned model brandishing
her tumbleweed high above her head,
leaking juice down a billowing black skirt
at that point where two parallel lines meet.

> *There the desert is flowering.*
> *There the desert bears fruit.*
> *There the sea is dead.*

## WAY OUT WEST

Suddenly war flares up
across the aisle. I am
eavesdropping, can't be sure . . .

Do you have your navy peacoat?
*Navy???* I don't *have* a navy coat.
     Crossfire. It must be the father now:
     Stop arguing.
     I'm not arguing.
     You're arguing right now.
     Because she said it was *navy*!

—So they are a family—

Though none of them has taken to looking like the others,
even after all these years. The mother is strung.
Her compulsive perm convinces no one of auburn.
Faded denim on the father voices contempt.
Nevertheless, his tender hand on the peacoat shoulder.

I start to think: what does it mean to lose a blue coat, not navy?

To ignore the speedometer?

To arrive a little late?

Or enjoy a bumper crop of zucchini,
somehow avoiding making one humiliating
Huge Loaf of It All—
    *zucchini*
    *eggs*
    *flour*
    *grudges*

*cinnamon*
    *brine* (he forgot the soda, bought powder instead)

Do they see me in the rearview mirror?
Fidget/trying not to/fix eyes on the fraying edges of
what little time we spend together
                        anymore.
Road trips not adventures.
Supper never dressed up as dinner.


I run into the (navy) fracas again in a public bathroom
and I think : this is what families do. They scrap.
They become less than themselves
in spite of themselves.
A fistful of backseat drivers
crushed behind the steering wheel.

*Lenox Lounge*
Who knew that, behind that flammable screen,
the coals were hurriedly swallowing roses. Whole.

<pre>
####
##@##
####
</pre>

*The Divine Lorraine*
Look on, you greedy nightmoths.
And learn what comes of flying
                    too close to the flame.
Consider the mounded ash:
the many wings once wrapped
in haughty silks.

<pre>
]]]    [[[
   {}
]]   [[
</pre>

*Saint Nick's*
RE: The danger is not that the wild Fire can storm [.-.| .-..-- | .-] across highways
like a wall of ochred water [..-.-.|-.], spewing the stinging brine of smoke.
The danger is that, years later, beneath the sooty footprints of retreating forests,
we ember-roses—all too quiet—will remember it [-.- |..-..|5 ♭3 4] like so many
                                                            *Yesterdays.*

## MARVIN IN STEREO/RIGHT EAR

When Marvin Gaye
was a little boy
he never dreamed in color.
His teachers thought that little
Marvin would never learn to spell.
       Ain't that peculiar, baby.

When Marvin was a boy,
his daddy whooped him hard.
He cried alone like a little girl
till sleep came and carried him home.
His daddy said he was just giving Marvin
       a sure foundation. His daddy swore

those whoopings hurt him
more than they hurt Marvin.

When Marvin was a boy,
he'd steal away, way out
                    where the river flows.

Then he'd sing like a girl.
He sang like a doo-wop band. He sang
like a tram run a red light. He'd sang

like a busted screen door. He'd be saaaanging
like the ocean sound like. He be saaaaahynging
like the noise over to the Ford factory.

When Marvin was a boy,
his daddy whooped him till he screamed.
When Marvin was a full-grown man,

his daddy shot him
for his own good.

## MORNING, 11.9.16

what sense makes death
a boon, booty grabbed
as we gape, dazed?
reality is an idiot
boxed in, trained to
contest nothing.　　　contest all.

in what sense will
we carry on, keep
calm, strum a lute,
beat a drum, dead?
next time death comes
knock-knock knocking us

let heaven demand our song:
now strangers to our homes.

# BURYING WILLIE, OUR LION

*for Bra' Willie, Keorapetse Kgositsile*

Well, sweet bean eater, you have come into your own.
Your new den is a chamber of light, thiefed
off of fat cats and liberated from the party magnates
with a prophet's right. With you there now, it is streaming
with the plenty that has always been enough.

We see you, sauntering among the lions and lionesses
nodding into each other's Solomonic eyes as you lie down
to watch us from your dearly won sanctuary. None
this side of ever will hold a candle to your pride.
But what you have given us: pride, paën, praise song,

such words must now arm us with the miracle of future memory.
We know how you be tonight, so we busy ourselves with your tasks:
clasping hands with prisoners, kissing cheeks of madmen,
spitting in the face of butchers, and dancing revolutions with Nina,
with Archie, with Jonas, A.B., Cassandra, Hugh, and Pharoah Sanders.

O Brother Willie, our own great lion: can you hear us
roaring in sorrowing rage at time's cruel trade?
to have known you, only to lose you,
only to gain your ancestral embrace,
our endless nobility, our most humble kin.

## MALICK SIDIBÉ'S CAMERA CALLS

Come to me, all you ochred yellows,
and you swaths of indigo-bled purple.
You, too poor for *boubous*
and you cotton blenders. Clutch
your full skirts, young women,
or smooth the curves of your *taille-basse*.
The negative will drain
whatever brassy print
your tailor settled on,
and wash your sun skin-bright.

The darker the room,
the groovier the glint
of a flirting eye, a glossed nail,
a lavish twist, done
just right. Night time is
the right time
to be young/gifted/and black,
to mash, grind,
funk up the checkered floor
and shake all living color
off, for the silvery surface of
infinity. Hang here

after the shoot, if you wish—
the beat goes on.

## LINGUA: GORGON

*now, for the silly*
*shot, pull a face,*
*screw up your eyes,*
*stick out your tongue.*

*light's dark purpose—never*
*cloaked in mystery—plays*
*hunter, taxidermy for tomorrow's*
*eyes. the camera will*

*not break: this portrait's*
*recto pose will freeze*
*your visage ever young.*
*stiff as stone this*

*will prove that you,*
*too, knew joy, chose*
*play, and shook a*
*head of serpents loose.*

# BENIN BRONZE

*after Elisabeth Frink*

Our face is one thick gild,
old metal screens our here.
Our now reflects your now: an
oily light besmears us all.
Live matter slicks our temples:
we are sheened.
We take umbrage, bronze it. We,
this brazen bloc. Night flares
to light our way and sear our nostrils.
Unthrown, we chase our golden-
blinkered lover. Justice stares
as if to meet our purple gaze.
Clavicle to clavicle, we
shall overcome this day.

## UNACCOMPANIED MINOR
Section 26, Kakuma Refugee Camp, Kenya, 1996

*after Robert Lyons, with Chinua Achebe*

Stand still in the hot shade, poised, sweatless.
See how the curtain sifts sand from sun
through paisley print.
See five orange lozenges
paint light onto his profile.

The thinker: here is a boy whose thighs have outgrown him.
Soon this neatly striped Old Navy shirt will not fit him either.

Notice that his shoes are still new enough
to stamp a grid on each resting place.
Let sentiment blur the outlines of a rondavel
through the curtain. Read a word, MASKANI, stamped
in stark, block capitals, as if on a ticket.

Fuss at the curtain, a veil against flies.
Count the trees here, as you lean against geometry.
Catch them catching the light, as you square the threshold.
Sense the slope of his cottoned shoulders,
the dance of print on skin. Know
his eyes are unquiet.
What is the name of the book in his hands,
his sanctum's seam, that wild unaccompanied
outer world, whose hem you may not mend?
Camp here, in this dwelling.

## CHILDREN'S SWINGS
Zinder, Niger, 1994

*after Robert Lyons, with Chinua Achebe*

Three slack wooden seats
bless the photographer
who left out the children's
bare bottoms. Against the wall
a bicycle leans, smug and real,
unwooden, unridden.
Its chain is ensconced in silky blue
painted metal. A yellow tangent
against green bars dust.
Above, the masjid's domes
fade, too serene to be
blue as well. The muezzin would
spill his nasal electric currents,
synthetic as wall plaster, if sight
were sound. Noiseless thorns and
weightless leaves surveille the wall. What
are they tracking? The ditch
below each swing is dug patiently
by the day labors of Chinese-made
children's shoes and patched with
blunt dry thorns. The light is slant,
the metal links hold fast.
In this land without rain, rust
harbors no intentions. Peace only.

## POND IN MUSEUM GARDEN

The too bright sky, the overexposed
blue. The lewd
round clouds, that naughty cherubic
bottom.

Roses are just pastel packets all balled up—
blousing cannas, playing salmon—
in December.
Staring into an oblong reflecting pool,

                  I still think:

                  *Lacquer black.*

                  *Aubergine.*

                  *Algae green.*

                  *An insect flays its circles assiduously.*
                  *A dead leaf, floating on poured navy.*

I looked down at myself.
None loved me back.
The pines on either side were long as El Greco.
Everything else is squat.

## RITUAL OBJECT

*after Willie Cole*


Through the artist's eyes,
we catch this breath of fire,
lifting water up to flight.
This dead weight sinks our histories
back into deep sleep, hidden away
to dream of      repair.

Waking, we clutch at the real
weight of a movable flood, catching
streams that pour through metal
still cold to the touch. Time
takes little care over us. Current
flowing, its song sighs across weft,
warp, wrinkle, fold. It collars us
in its              minutiae.


Iron, pierced for steam's escape!
Ease across what was once shift,
now skirt, scarf, shirt sleeve, sheet.
Warm what will soon cool.
Stiffen what will turn soft.
Smooth our way, and drape us
in the dignity of
                  this new day.

# THE BODY COUNTS

The body count at Lockerbie.
The body count in the London bombing.

The body count at Tiananmen Square.
The body count at Sharpeville. Then Soweto.

The body count in Chicago on any given day.
The body count in New Orleans on that particular day.

The body count in West, Texas, or in Boston. Burying
Tamerlan's body counts against the undertaker from Virginia.

The body count at dawn in Waziristan, that very same week.
The body count at an Afghan wedding, collateral.

The body counts to the mother, cradling her bloodstained daughter, just born.
The body counts to the mother, cradling her bloodstained daughter, just dead.

The body count here, in Philadelphia, city of brotherly love. Under rubble, North, West.

The body count by classroom, children caned to death over Bokassa's school uniforms.
The body counts in garment factories, in strawberry fields, in the mines.

The body count at Jonestown, that matched the Kool-Aid cup count.
The body count at Little Big Horn, and then at Wounded Knee.

The body count according to Ida B. Wells. Sweet Jesus.
The body count according to the Khmer Rouge.

The body count, not including Habayarimana.
The body counts not mentioned.

The body count at Gettysburg—
The body counts before:

onboard,          over,
then below.

\*

The body
counts to Elinore, visiting Emil's grave four birthdays since. She
brings him flowers, and a blanket embroidered with the periodic table to warm his grave.
She tends the land that hugs him as if it were her own broken
body.

## WILDCAT

*after Kahlil Joseph*

Cicadas echo the *sha sha sha* that consoled the homesick.
Enter the drone:              the presence of the present.
Still, here, behind a veil,        far from Du Bois country
grief empties a man's pockets.

You hear angels when there's no one there
Through a thick lens,      you spy innocence.
Light resurrects her, girdled in geomancy's truth.
Slant light slips away.

What do the innocent have to do with angels?
What does an angel carry in her purse?
What sly joy surprises an innocent?
What terror? Yesterday's flaming wood,

is metal now, fencing the beastly off from man.
This snare again flaying black skin, once more
excruciation casts the human beyond its frontier.

Cow boys, grown sons of light and darkness
stand guard at the boundary
between cattle and men.

How do you turn an animal loose?
Do you run alone, when you run free?
I am the darker brother
bordering nation, side-eying freedom.

*I am* the darker brother.
Girding your loins
with truth, tell nothing
but the whole truth, slant.

Ghosts dance like this, mercifully still:
once this was Indian territory. Wingless
flight brought them here to douse the wood.

The harmonies haven't changed.
Remember the land.
Remember the body.
Remount the horse.

Get right back on
the frontier:
flesh against flesh
black skin against hide.

What must the innocents never know?
        Where they may roam and what is out of bounds.
And if they lose their way?
        When did innocence ever kiss a black cheek?
Who stands guard lest Beauty, the innocent's alias, give the slip?

        A voice was heard in Ramah, lamentation's
        bitter consolation: the innocent
        are not. Angels look away. The taking is
        too soon. Ramallah's grief sealed off.

Through this dark lens, wind cannot shield
the rain's face, a blur of tears. You look like
my brother, only darker. Goggle truth in
this opaque vision, our only correction. Still
someone rises. Still someone's left behind.
Someone's crying

lord

how quiet it is, up in here

feels like a ghost town.

What's held is sacred.

you walking towards me:
don't perspire/how *you* doin'/all homegirl like.

you walking past me:
huh, not my turn today.

you all friendly, walking against the line, fucking it all up:
you fucking up the flow, man.

you picking out that tight brunette, flirting through a broken window:
theater in the round, man, theater in the fuckin' round.

you not getting her number:
i know, i know, it wasn't about that.

surprise, surprise. you walking up to the four brown brothas:
everybody sees it, everybody knows.

you asking all friendly officer-like/what brings you to austin:
watch list.

them closing ranks, bro-muttering. big bro-muffling/it is what it is:
flash them a smile/it gets old, don't it?

getting loud about football, with an all-american swagger/he's a conservative quarterback:
whoa, blank look, almost cold. solidarity don't come that cheap.

the whole line watching the instructional video, shot live:
nothing, absolutely nothing.

the video screen retroactively calling this a checkpoint:
officer, i see two armed officers perched up there ready to snipe.

ain't nothing else on:
ain't nothing else on.

america:
america god shed his light.

a crowded airport:
this shit gets old.

if you see something:
say something.

# LINGUA: QUICK-TONGUED

*Mind your p's, watch*
*your q's, don't let*
*that slip, don't fork,*
*don't double-tongue, don't*
*twist the words right*

*out of your mouth.*
*A sharp word can*

*kill. A hanged tongue*
*turns purple, swollen, lewd.*
*The smell of barbecue*
*ribs, strange fruit, will*
*never be the same.*

## BALLADE: THYROID GOES ROGUE

Thyroid breaks formation, as
moth flees cocoon. Then
it spreads; wings it.
Thyroid flits through every

last metaphysical problem, blade-
rolling at a party.
It's 1999, literally. Thyroid
toys with my heart,

wrenches my little gut,
pops eyes, grabs my
hair, including my legs—
skinny shin shinned. So

I have never shaved.
Thyroid fucks me over
and over again. Checking
out of the funny

house or pages, leaving
looney toons behind, I
heard the door about
to slam, getting caught.

Then: *By the way,*
*Thyroid really hates you.*
*So do we, so*
*we just left Thyroid*

*at your throat. If*
*you want to get*

*over this, check it*
*out.* Weeks later a

bill arrived by mail.
Thyroid nasty. Thyroid wild.
Thyroid run on no
sleep and swell up

a stiff stench in
every joint that gives.
Thyroid beat me. Thyroid
rage, but only my

eyes were to be
believed. Thyroid make me
so mad I slam the
door my damn self.

Shit storm: now it's
snowing outside. My friend
is home. I crash
but I can't stay

here forever. So I
opt to go north.
It's a black thang.
Bakered back, I go

to Saint Elizabeth's instead.
Luckily, I guess, this
po-po siren ride is
free. So I die

down with Jesus for
the traditional three day
nap. No afro-pick provided.
Back on the road

to healthy living, I
crawl into a womb—
chair rocking in Wellington,
Ohio, home of the

biggest KKK club this
side of Kiwanis. All
twelve Baker kids come
rotating through. All blonde

and blue-eyed as their
Irish Catholic grand dad.
All good. I choose
my ex's womb: his

moms and I drive
to East Side Cleveland:
that's Not Shaker Heights.
Up in their house,

renovation is a way
of life, of living
here, now, with black
folk on all sides.

\*

One zap and Thyroid
gone. Dead, weight withered
out of sight. Throat
cleared. This song was

caught twenty years ago.
Now I must sing
out, unburied moth dust.
O sing, rust-rotted throat!

# THREE INTERMEZZI FOR UNACCOMPANIED THYROID

*1*
Bromide cleans,
browns you.

*2*
The thyroid,
laid low.

*3*
Well, it's
not cancer.

That's good.

## MISTERIOSO: IODINE 131 MEETS THE ROYAL THYROID

All around is humming.
Wood never waits quietly.

LaMonte was in Dakota. Young, that is.
That was what the dear one loved.

After dark we all fall down
—or go home now. That was South Dakota,

or maybe just blossomed potatoes.
I forget now.                    The buzz

was for tuning, to flatten the moth's tumor.
That's all gone now. Like bromides.

What was it she meant when she rasped:
*The bromeliads drip amber, and it all slides down—easy.*

CADENZA: THYROID RIDES AGAIN

Most X-rays reverse
light, or mess with
it. I mean, the
bones stay white, cracks

look back, looking black,
but you have to
back light them to
get any information out

of them. So blood
work works better. Suppose
you are sick and
tired, mostly of not

sleeping because your body
won't tire of you.
Suppose it's 1998, not
yet even party time.

Suppose doctor says—*Well!*
*you don't want to*
*lose your eyes, do*
*you? Do you really*

*plan to let Thyroid*
*attack your only heart?*
Instead you let them
radiate your future

into a lifelong relationship
with Synthroid. *Oh settle*
*down. In a few*
*years they will show*

*real class and put*
*a check in the*
*mail. Courting? No. "Thanks*
*for the cash. Here's*

*a coupon."** Offer only
good if you signed
the paper work when
the possible effects were

just radiant. Now is
like that, but not.
The books said you
would glow. Well, you

do look like you're
turning red. Any how,
Graves sometimes does return.
Sometimes it bakes into

that bun in the oven.
These middle wives would
like to check on
you, these twenty years

since. These would like
to care for you.
Mama, this love note
is for you. Sweetie.

# KOAN OF THE GREAT CAT

*for Zarina, faithful teacher*

I bow before the patience of the cat.
Never known to cower before
anything but rain, hers is the roost,
and mine, the pen. We crowd into
each other's warmth, vie for sun, and squint
according to our species, slant. Though she
glances away, I risk the same old gesture:
trust. I handle fur far richer than
anything I own, but this soft self
I claim as my true luxury, pure silk.

Wild pride, my most selfish crime!
Her claw, her tooth, her tail, her lesson:
the antidote to love pressed
is love's sharp requite.

## LINGUA: BABBLE

*into language,* dada *first—*
*no slight to* mama,
*merely shape of tongue—*
*soft palate's* papa *slips*
*into sense and out*
*with play of lips*
*and dimpled cheeks. say*
baba, *baby, say* abu,
*say* yaye, *say* ma mère,
*say* mamam, *reach*
*for milk, for breast,*
*for animal parts so*
*lately found. where nipple*
*played coquette, call her*
mammal, *this wild wet*
*nurse whose language coos,*
*and cuddles, clings to*
*you, slumps helpless into*
*slumber's arms, then starts*
*at the beginner's stuttering*
*language, say just enough.*

## STUMBLING BLOCK

His one and only
son, sweet mama's boy,
X'd out on wood
for such as these?
This is wondrous strange—

what careless mystery! Some
spider's net to snatch
a mother's throat and
strangle praise—past understanding.
Give us *peace* instead.

## BOY LOTUS

I am still
young enough to
have the sense to ask:
why lilies? why purple,
or red, or blue? why
this monkish code?

I am still
wide-eyed and eager to
drink the dishwater,
wear only dresses,
and grasp the mysteries
of flat bread.

If you steal from me now
I will always be a beggar,
wild-eyed and raw. And
if you do not take this from me
I will always be a beggar,
harvesting other men's stems.

# INFINITIVE

*We believed because we saw. Bless the others.*


To hear a grown man weeping
In the thin, high voice of laughter
with a ghostly guest, in careful
seduction of layer upon layer
of dirt, slipped on. An unwashed man,
smelling himself—death's stale stink—
not once, not twice, but a legion of
scabs, scrawled across his skin, or
just below, feasting on his slotted
veins, mapping the way to his heart.

To hear this man shouting dislocated
stories, conjugated in a thousand voices,
each time the same old same old,
each time a different teller, so that
he who is one becomes many, and
they call him Legion. Each new bass
declares the hidden truth is a lie,
each hearing leaves the audience
uneasy, confused but not rebuked.
To laugh under breath. To laugh in his face.

To hear that man chink metal against
metal's legion chains, unbroken, then
burst rabid and without words. To
see him break their bite, and fear.
To hear the frenzy growing louder,
and dread a Samson tale. To watch him
gripped by empty skies, roving among
empty graves, staring blank as a leopard

stretched out on a branch, scanning
the dark outline of hill against untimely night.

To hear that man laughing, openly, against
the double ban of cackle and of shame
that sullied his good name; the rustle as
he fumbles through the night
shade, grasping for a jagged stone
or fistfuls, enough for legions. To mistake
the next sound for hunter gripping
mountain ram, then catch the giggle,
and crackle of fire, the glint of scarlet
streaming from his wrists, his chest, his spine.

To hear this man, these men, these legions
outraged at one man's intimacy, whimpering
to mute his sentence. To look away. To listen
in on that wheeling deal: freedom for a
straitjacket. To hear a squeal rise up
across the way, like a slaughterhouse, where
legioned swine as filthy as a woman's blood
suddenly amplified to demonic screams. To hear
the chorus speeding toward the gorge's lip.
To watch that man spell his first word: mercy.
To see him clothed, bright, clean,
and in his own right mind.

## TRIPTYCH

*The lesson of the first murderer:*
Anger will eat you live. Anger
will undo you. Anger will split
you wide open like firewood
before it's dry.

*The lesson of the second murderer:*
Nietzsche, though belated, did
arrive at a truth: the divine is long
gone. Our time, as all time,
holds little sacred.

*The lesson of the third murderer:*
Draw near to a god and chances are,
that god will draw near to you.
It's never too late to
crash a party,

# WHEN THOMAS FINALLY ROLLED UP, I SAID

What I been through down there?
I tell you, my own sweet Thomas, it ain't
nothing I would wish on my wors'
enemy. Now you know I've been
laid low before, but this? Good god
almighty, this was deep, man—
it was heavy underground.

Give me some skin, brother T!
Now, you know you wrong for that.
See here, the nail cut a hole
clear to the other side. It'll grow back.
Show me your stupid secret handshake.
Hug me tight, Thomas, hold me close
and hug my neck. My side still not right.
For real? I wasn't sure I'd make it back.

Thomas, I'm a tell you this straight
up: I would lay down my life—hell,
I would spill my thick red blood—
before I'd let my mamma go
through what I felt deep down in there.
You wanna talk about a stench? All
I could smell was cold, hard doubt.

Look—Death ain't a thing to visit with,
you don't just go, come back, and tell.
It was a whole different kind of lonesome,
man. That's a trip I won't take twice. But
Thomas, my main man, I got up! I still high!
I am here, sweet brother T. Good god,
I'm here to stay.

## FACING EL GRECO

Those wonders that cannot be unlearned,
halcyon light glinting through a renaissance
playing with shade and colors I remember
as my own: the scarlet tumble of fragrant rose-leaf,
showered on Whitsunday from rooftop peepholes
—window stains suddenly scented, seized by faith;
the organ's orders, O phantasmic demon flying in the face
of mechanics, outpacing the grave language of science
and the apple's Fall, echoing synthesizers before
the end of the age of the wheel, beating time out of joint.

Try as I might, the alchemy of wood on silver
comes back to me, mumbling some gnostic spell
between the lewd fact of birth and the Roman
priesthood, after the Turkish crossroad. How it reminds
me of other stains, wood, nixes, reason circled
and mind transferred to body, bread, tongues, and
even a ghost held holy: how metaphor's procession
anchors every revolution, centers the perpendicular.

So concede this to the people of grey and brown
wool, that itchy irritant. Grant those who eat meat
past its prime, suffer wind's stridency, know too little
of spice, yet haunt the foreign middle, this revel
in the psychedelic stretch of bodies:
a Greek canvas
rambling between
Venice and Toledo.

## WE ARE THE DARKER SISTER.

O God who saw fit to print me
long after silver's gelatin age:
you have etched *us* in cursive
cipher. Lived in negative,
we exalt its secret revelations:
a hairpin fracture spinning light
through wounded bone, the cry of
that cryptic wilderness, the body.
O you, whose wisdom is taken
for hysteria in the measured mind,
why did you give the scramblers pens,
and us, this flash of song and lightning's
tale, too soon muted in memory's churn?
How are we to spell this velvet touch
of ours, sun-burnished Mother?

ACKNOWLEDGMENTS

My thanks to the editors of the following publications, in which these poems first appeared, sometimes in slightly different versions.

*Africa Is a Country* website, January 2018: "Burying Willie, Our Lion" (as "Willie, Our Lion").

*African Literature Today* 34 (2016): "Benin Bronze"; "Manual for Initiation into the Zebra Sisterhood"; "Ethiopia Stretches Forth Her Hands" (as "The Not-Jobbing Blues").

*Beating the Graves* (University of Nebraska Press, 2017): "Prelude to a Kiss."

*Center for Book Arts Broadsides Series* (2004): "Way Out West" (as "The Seat in Front of Me").

*Harvard Review Online* (February 2018): "On the Isle of Lesbos."

*Illuminations* (Spring 2015): "Electioneered" (as "Elections").

*InTensions*, 5 (Fall/Winter 2011): "Autumn Leaves."

*Meridians* 17, no. 2 (November 2018). "And They Didn't Die."

*New Coin Poetry* 53, no. 2 (December 2017): "First Guardian of Flight: *The Angel of Time*" and "Second Guardian of Flight: *The Angel of Refinement*" (as "Guardians of Flight"); "Profile."

*New Orleans Review* 43 (2017): "Blue Note."

*Ngugi: Reflections on His Life of Writing* (Boydell & Brewer, 2018): "A Song at Dawn."

Poem-a-Day, American Academy of Poets (May 14, 2018): "Ritual Object."

*Supplement* (Fall 2016): "at war"; "Tell me something good."

*women: poetry: migration [an anthology]* (Theenk Press, 2017): "How I write"; "Our Mother of Stone."